For

THAT SPECIAL

Friend

A Token of Love

by Suzanne Siegel Zenkel

Designed by Michel Design
Illustrated by Grace De Vito

PETER PAUPER PRESS, INC.
WHITE PLAINS·NEW YORK

For Paula

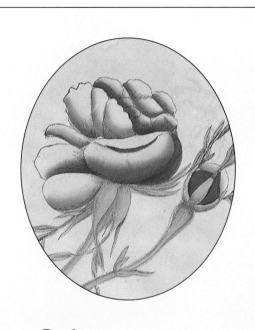

*You'll have the whole world
in your hands if you can count a
friend on each finger.*

A person can always be your
friend, even if she is not a friend
in all ways.

*D*on't just dream of the person
you'd like to be.
Become that person.

Allow your friend to make mistakes, and give yourself the same freedom.

Accept affection with open arms, and give it with an open heart.

*Sow the seeds of friendship
and your garden will be
forever green.*

*Isn't it strange that the busiest
women always seem to have the
most time for other people?*

*When regarding
a friend,
look for someone who is
a friend to herself,
for she will invariably
be a friend to you.*

The greatest wonder of friendship is that the more you give, the richer you grow.

※—◦—※

A woman's life can be measured not by the amount of wealth she has accumulated, but by the quality and duration of her friendships.

nine

*O*ne true friend is worth a
hundred casual acquaintances.

*A*ttitude is everything.

*W*e may dwell on different
shores, but in the end we are all
in the same boat.

An achievement is so much sweeter when celebrated with a close friend.

twelve

*Look at things with a cool head
and a warm heart.*

*In the tournament of life,
the real trophy is a trustworthy
friend.*

*A friend's worth is not in the
value of what she has, but rather
in what she is.*

To share your thoughts with
a trusted friend is to double
your happiness and halve
your troubles.

Why look in the distance to
find happiness? The secret lies in
extracting simple pleasures from
everyday life.

fifteen

It's awfully nice to have a friend who'll bask in your sunshine—even nicer, though, to have one who'll help you find your way through the darkness.

Your todays will be happier if you cease to dwell on what happened yesterday or on what may come tomorrow.

*Of all the world's wonders,
none rises to so heavenly a plane
as that of a true and lasting
friendship.*

*A friend is like crystal.
Handle with care.*

*Friendships, like good wine,
need time to age before one can
savor and enjoy their flavor.*

You are twice blessed if you can travel the journey of life with a true friend.

*Sharing dark thoughts with a
friend lightens your heart and
turns night to day.*

*Don't confuse living as you
want to live with asking others to
live as you do. The first is self-
assurance, the second, self-
importance.*

*ℬe a friend and you'll
have a friend.*

*𝒫rize your new friends,
and cherish the old.*

*𝒮hould you find fault with a
friend, convey it quietly, but
should you have praise for her, by
all means proclaim it publicly.*

twenty one

If you nurture a friendship
with love and care, that
friendship will flourish in untold
ways.

*G*uilt should not be the
motivator of good acts. Treat
others as you would like to be
treated and your good acts will
flow naturally.

*Sometimes the most valuable
thing a friend can lend is
a ready ear.*

*A friend feels good when
her friend feels good.*

*The only plane on which
friendship can thrive is an
equal plane.*

Laughter is a vital force in life and in friendship. If you remember one thing only, remember to seize every opportunity to have a good laugh.

❖❖❖

A great friend, whatever her circumstances, wishes you the best.

*$\mathcal{P}$ride
yourself on
being able to
give good advice
to a friend, but
even more in
knowing how to
accept it.*

*B*eware: Too often a single cutting word can sever the bonds of friendship.

*Y*ou can't be all things to all people and still be yourself.

*I*f all the world's a stage, try to cast your friends in leading roles.

A comfortable silence shared
by friends speaks volumes.

When your own strength
falters, lean on a friend's
sympathetic shoulder.

$\mathscr{F}$riends outlast trends.

$\mathscr{U}$nderstanding makes
differences disappear.

$\mathscr{W}$hen you cease to have
friends, you cease to live.

twenty nine

Find a friend in yourself.

Laughter and compassion are two vital building blocks of friendship, but loyalty is the cement that seals the bond.

Between good friends, the books are never balanced.

Giving in to friendly persuasion can be more satisfying than getting your own way.

Don't let anger stand in the way. Remember, friendships need to be nurtured with forgiveness.

The roaring
brook
The whispering
pine
The cooing birds
A friend by your
side

Renewing a long-dormant friendship can be more enriching than cultivating a new friend.

True friends delight in each other's successes and support each other in times of sorrow.

thirty five

May all your days be just like you —filled with warmth and love.

*M*ake friends by being true.
Keep them by being loyal.

*L*ike a flower, friendship
blossoms over time.

$\mathcal{D}$on't let the past discourage
you. Embrace new opportunities
and discover a rewarding future.

$\mathcal{F}$riends can laugh at
themselves—and at each other!

*Compassion
is the essential
link in the
chain of
humanity.*

forty

*There's no more effective cure
for loneliness than time spent
with a good friend.*

*Like a good book, a lasting
friendship has many chapters.*

$\mathcal{B}$e yourself. It's not easy pretending to be someone else.

$\mathcal{T}$he road of life is what you make of it, but it sure helps to have good friends along the way.

forty three

*Bury the hatchet and unearth
the joy of an old friendship.*

*Be tolerant of your friends.
Even the pick of the bunch
sometimes has a few blemishes.*

To dwell on a friend's mistake is to make a second mistake.

Friends are like precious gems; treasure them and they will sparkle.

A lasting friendship is marked not so much by a sprinkling of grand gestures as by a long stream of small kindnesses.

forty seven

An outstretched hand is often
an invitation to an open heart.

It is easier to reach the
mountaintop if you get an
occasional push from a friend.

Like ripe summer fruit, a good friendship should be properly preserved.

Good friends respond without being called.

Friends drop in when others drop out.

Laughter is contagious. Make sure you get your daily dose!

A friendship rooted in trust sprouts branches of love.

Sometimes friends have to pass the peace pipe just to clear the smoke.

A friend yesterday, a friend
today, a friend tomorrow—
though not always
the same friend.

⋖⋗⟶●⟵⋖⋗

*V*ariety is the spice of life.
Pepper yours with many friends.

If you open your eyes and
heart to all people, you will be
blessed with many good friends.

A budding friendship warms
like a ray of sun and awakens
in our hearts the joy of a
brand new day.

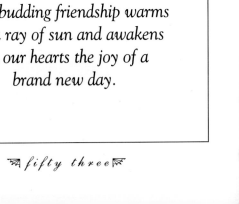

Friendship can endure over many years, even when the content of that friendship changes greatly.

Drink from the cup of friendship, and it will never need replenishment.

You see only
your most beautiful
self reflected in the
eyes of a true
friend.

Aim for the stars and you'll find a galaxy of success.